Everybody Feels...

Angry

Jane Bingham

QED Publishing

This edition published 2012 for Index Books

First published in the UK in 2006 by QED Publishing
A Quarto Group company
230 City Road
London ECIV 2TT

www.qed-publishing.co.uk

Reprinted in 2011

A Catalogue record for this book is
available from the British Library.

ISBN 978 1 84538 723 5

Written by Jane Bingham
Designed by Alix Wood
Editor Clare Weaver
Illustrations Helen Turner

Printed in China

Contents

Feeling angry

People have lots of different **feelings**.

Sometimes, they feel happy and **calm**.

Sometimes, they feel angry.

How do you think Kate feels now?

Everyone has times when
they feel angry. When was
the last time you felt angry?

How does it feel?

When you get angry, a very strong feeling **bubbles up** inside you.

It can make you feel **shaky** and hot.

Sometimes, being angry makes you want to cry.

Sometimes, it makes you want to

SHOUT OUT LOUD.

Being angry doesn't feel good.

Luckily, this feeling doesn't last **forever**.

What makes you angry?

All sorts of things make people feel angry.

Here's what happened to Jessie and Tom.

Tom's story

My name is Tom.

One morning, Spiffy was sick in my school bag.

It was disgusting!

Mum made me use one of
my sister's bags instead.

I HATE PINK!

On the way to school, a bus **whizzed** past me...

I got covered in mud.

When I got to school, everybody laughed at me.

I felt so angry,
I thought I
would **BURST**.

I told my best friend to go away and NOT COME BACK!

Jessie's story

I'm Jessie.

One day, I wanted to ride my bike.

But Mum said I had to come inside.

Then I asked Henry to play a game with me.

But he said he was much too **busy**.

Then I started to paint a picture.
But Dad said it was time for bed.

I went to bed in a very **BAD MOOD!**

The next day when I got to school, I still felt angry.

Then I saw Tom, and we started to talk.

18

We talked about our angry feelings.

Talking together made us feel much calmer.

Feeling sorry

*Sometimes when you're angry, you say things you don't really **mean**.*

*Later, you feel **sorry** for what you said.*

Saying sorry makes everyone feel better.

I'm sorry.

Glossary

bad mood if you're in a bad mood, everything makes you feel angry and upset

bubbles up when a feeling bubbles up inside you, it becomes stronger and stronger until you have to let it out

burst when something bursts, it breaks apart suddenly

busy if you're busy, you have lots of things to do

calm if you're calm, you feel peaceful and you don't worry about anything

feelings your feelings tell you how you are and what kind of mood you're in

forever if something goes on forever, it never ends

mean if you mean to do something, you plan to do it

shaky if you're shaky, you don't feel very strong and sometimes you can't stop your arms or legs from wobbling

sorry if you're sorry about something, you feel sad about it

whizz when something whizzes, it goes very fast

Index

Notes for parents and teachers

- Look at the front cover of the book together. Talk about the picture. Can your children guess what the book is going to be about? Read the title together.

- Read the first line on page 4: 'People have lots of different feelings.' Help your children to make a list of different feelings.

- Ask your children to draw some simple faces showing different feelings. Then talk about them. Which feelings make them feel good? Which don't feel so good?

- Talk about what happens to Kate on pages 4–5. Discuss Kate's feelings – first, when she is enjoying her ice cream, and then when her little brother takes it away.

- Ask your children if they think it's all right to be angry. Help your children to think about times when being angry is the right response.

- Read the question on page 5: 'When was the last time you felt angry?' Talk with your children about times when they have felt angry.

- Read about how it feels to be angry (pages 6–7). Ask your children to draw a picture of how it feels.

- Read page 8, and look at the picture of Kate feeling better. Ask your children how they think Kate feels now. Can your children remember times when they were angry, but later they felt better?

- Read the first part of Tom's story together (pages 10–12). Ask your children how they think Tom feels. Talk about how it feels when lots of things go wrong.

- Read pages 13–14 together. Then ask some questions: Was Tom was right to be angry? Was he right to shout at his best friend?

- Read the first part of Jessie's story (pages 15–17). Was Jessie right to feel angry? How do your children think the people in her family felt?

- Role-play being Jessie and her brother Henry. Ask your children to take turns at being Jessie (who wants Henry to play with her) and Henry (who is busy at his computer). How do your children think Henry feels?

- Look at the last part of Jessie and Tom's story (pages 18–19). Talk about why they started to feel better.

- Look at pages 20–21 together. Then talk about feeling sorry. Help your children to think about times when they should say sorry, and times when they don't need to feel sorry. Should Tom say sorry to his best friend?

- Ask your children to remember a time when they said sorry. How did saying sorry make them feel?